REVISED EDITION

The EYFS Inspection in practice

The step-by manage y

ce

By Jenny Ba

Published by Practical Pre-School Books, A Division of MA Education Ltd, St Jude's Church, Dulwich Road, Herne Hill, London, SE24 0PB
Tel: 0207 738 5454
www.practicalpreschoolbooks.com
© 2009 MA Education Ltd. Revised edition 2012.
Front cover photo by Lucie Carlier, © 2012 MA Education Ltd.
Illustrated by Cathy Hughes.

The EYFS Inspection in practice ISBN 978-1-909101-04-3

Introduction

This book, fully revised with the 2012 EYFS guidance, is designed to support you in the completion of your Self-Evaluation Form (SEF) and help you to make the most of your Ofsted inspection.

The SEF has received a mixed reception, but this book aims to explain and show its comprehensive value. It is set out in clear chapters to guide you through the processes of the inspection, with checklists and reference charts for you and your staff to to work through.

We begin with reflective practice, as this is an essential tool for continual development within a setting, both for individuals and the setting as a whole. The skills and awareness that are honed through reflective practice will support both the completion of the SEF and, going forward, looking at how to develop practice following your inspection.

The chapter on the SEF has a comprehensive grids, guiding you through each section of the SEF with suggestions and points for consideration to help you complete the SEF relevantly and constructively. These grids provide a much fuller explanation of the questions posed in the Ofsted Early Years Self Evaluation Guidance document. Additionally, there are suggestions for evidence that you could make available to back up your statements.

We then move onto other preparations you may need to make for an inspection: your general principles of good practice for all visitors to your setting and the involvement of all practitioners working in the setting. These are explored in the chapters 'First impressions count' and 'Preparing for your inspection.' A first impressions checklist will help you to objectively look at supporting your own setting and identify how a visitor might see it.

The chapter 'The inspection day' explores how to cope on the day and support staff as well as the importance of paying close attention to the feedback you receive from the inspector. 'After the inspection' looks at how you can take your practice forward and move on, regardless of your grading outcome.

This book is designed to enable anyone working in the early years, be as a childminder, nursery nurse or reception teacher, to make their EYFS inspection a positive and stress-free experience.

Reflective practice

In the DfES publication 'Key Elements for Effective Practice' (2005), it states that:

'Effective practice in the early years requires committed, enthusiastic and reflective practitioners with a breadth and depth of knowledge, skills and understanding.'

Additionally in the Ofsted publication 'Childcare groups: a passion to be outstanding' (2009) it states that:

'Outstanding providers told us that reflective practice is crucial to their success. They are not complacent but aspire continually to do better. They regularly review what they do and how this helps children.'

For a long time it has been considered good practice for practitioners to 'reflect on their own practice'. It is a phrase widely used, but what does it mean exactly and how should we reflect? There are in fact two terms that you should be familiar with: reflective practice and reflective practitioners.

Reflective practice

This means thinking about and analysing your actions and practice with a view to changing, developing and improving practice.

Reflective practitioner

This describes a practitioner who is aware of their strengths and skills, as well as their knowledge gaps and areas for skill development – and are ready to work on them.

So, it is not just being aware of what you do and what your strengths and skills are, it is about taking action and moving forward. It is about identifying what you could do differently, how you could better support the children and work more effectively with your team.

There are many benefits to reflective practice and being a reflective practitioner.

Benefits for the individual include:

- Skills are developed.

- More motivated.

- Greater job satisfaction.

- Personal development.

- Become an agent of change.

- Better able to meet the needs of children and their families.

- More confident.

- Able to meet challenges presented within the job role.

- Stronger professional relationships within the team.

Benefits for the children:

- Their individual needs are more likely to be effectively met.

- The learning environment will better meet their needs.

- Practitioners have a greater understanding of how to support their development.

Benefits for the setting:

- A more effective setting with highly skilled and motivated staff.

- Staff feel more valued.

- Children are happy and settled as their needs are met and supported, leading to happy parents and a good reputation for the setting.

- More organised and efficient.

- Staff become agents of change and ensure that the setting is constantly evolving and developing.

The setting is perceived to be innovative with a focused vision.

So the benefits may well be numerous, but how do you start to be a reflective practitioner? For purposeful and effective reflective practice, we need to invest time in the process, so that it becomes part of everyone's way of working.

Most people are already doing it without realising it. The observations we carry out, the reflection on children's needs and interests and how we use that information to inform planning are all partial reflections, and the skills honed through that practice can help us to be good 'reflectors'.

We need to begin assessing ourselves, the need to do what we do and how we do it; remembering to be completely truthful. Reflective practice is never going to be truly effective unless we are 100% honest with ourselves about what we do, remembering there is a distinct difference between what we might say or think we do and what we actually do. Reflection is like putting a mirror up to your work and seeing from the reverse viewpoint what you are doing.

Some practitioners may need additional support to look clearly into the mirror, and identify what it is they say they do and what they actually do. This necessary support will largely depend on their learning style and ability to objectively analyse.

Let's begin with some straightforward basic questions about ourselves as positive role models and then move on to our knowledge, awareness and understanding of individual key children.

Reflect on your practice in relation to these questions about being a positive role model; remember to ask yourself – be honest and truthful.

- I always say hello and good morning to the people around me.

- I offer to help other staff members set up or tidy away.

- I always say please and thank you.

- I am patient.

- I like to help people.

- I listen to other people's points of view.

- I am tidy and organised.

Having done that, you can then move on to thinking about a specific child. Your perception might be, as with the questions above, that you do that all the time, but do you? Choose one of your key children as an example:

How often do you smile and acknowledge the child positively?

How much time do you spend listening to and talking to the child?

What type of activities does the child enjoy most?

How do you use these activities to help the child learn?

Having eased yourself in, you can then begin to delve into specific aspects of your work using the following techniques to help you gain an insight.

- To begin with, you need to question what you do, why you do it and how you do it. Then think about your thoughts and responses. This might be done individually or as a team.

- Could it be done differently: are there alternatives that could be better or more effective? Ask 'what if?'. Test new ideas, maybe visit other settings to gain a different insight and perspective.

- Remember to be open-minded: don't just assume a new way of doing something won't necessarily work, have a go and see what happens, you might be surprised.

- As you seek alternatives consider the different points of views of those involved/affected e.g. parents, children, other staff.

- Use reflective practice to identify and resolve problems, using a problem solving approach.

There are many aspects of practice that can be considered e.g. partnership with parents, snack time, management of behaviour, hygiene routines, child initiated opportunities in the outside environment.

EYFS Themes

EYFS Theme: A Unique Child

What activities or experiences in the setting help children to think about:

- The things that make them feel good about themselves?

- The people who help them?

- How to keep themselves safe?

- How to recognise and avoid possible danger?

- Reasons for making particular choices?

- The reason they are allowed to do or to have some things and not other things?

EYFS Theme: Enabling Environments

- How well do you reflect examples of outdoor learning in your observations and assessments of children?

- Does indoor provision meet the needs of all the children as both a place to feel at home and a place to learn?

- How do you ensure that the deployment of staff is flexible enough to respond to the flow and movement of children between indoors and outdoors?

EYFS Theme: Creating and thinking critically

- What open-ended activities do you provide for children in your setting?

- Do you give children the experience of playing with paint and glue before expecting them to use them to make a Christmas card?

- Have you ever recorded your interactions with children to see how you support the development of creativity and critical thinking?

To gain a clearer insight into specific aspects of practice, you could work through the questions outlined in photocopiable sheets at the end of this chapter or refer to the text boxes with lists of questions.

Supporting your team

- How do you ensure that team members understand their roles and responsibilities?

- How do you support members of the team in their work?

- Do you actively recognise an individual's strengths?

- How often do you provide feedback on staff performance?

- How do you ensure that their work is interesting and valuable?

- Do you encourage team members to take on responsibility?

- How do you ensure that team members are able to extend their knowledge, skills and experience?

- Do you act upon things that have been said to you, are you seen as being pro-active?

- What opportunities have you provided for staff to contribute new ideas and develop their capabilities?

It isn't sufficient to simply ask the questions and reflect on your practice: you then have to take action to develop practice and move forward. You need to identify how this can be done, who will need to be involved and whether any additional support or training will be required.

Keeping records of discussions on reflective practice and documenting how you are going to move forward, shows good practice in relation to self-assessment.

This can be done in two ways, as the individual or the team/setting as a whole. Records kept as part of the appraisal and supervision process will show how the individual is a reflective practitioner. For the team or setting as a whole, the easiest way to do this is to complete an action plan, identifying what you need to develop in terms of practice. The targets set in the action plan must be **SMART**:

Specific – clearly identified as actions.

Measurable – it must clearly show it can be seen that the actions have been achieved or not.

Achievable – practitioners can work easily to achieve them.

Realistic – all the necessary tools need to be available so the actions can be achieved.

Time bound – a date identified when the actions need to be achieved by or identifying when there will be a review.

The photocopiable sheet on page 6 shows a reflective practice action plan.

Failing to act upon what has been identified through reflective practice can have a demotivating effect, so the follow through action is essential. This is particularly important for managers supporting practitioners in the setting.

As practitioners become more aware and reflective practice skills are developed, they may wish to keep a reflective practice diary. This type of diary can be a record of what is useful to you and a memory cue. It may describe significant incidents relating to practice and facilitate evaluation of these incidents and implications for practice.

Becoming a reflective practitioner as previously stated gives a much clearer insight into a individual's role, and once this insight has evolved, more searching questions can be asked.

- How do I see my role?

- What kind of practitioner do I think I am: what are my key skills and strengths?

- What are my personal thoughts on the role of early years education?

- How do I show that I am consistent at all times in my practice?

Once reflective practice becomes integral to what happens within the setting, the benefits will quickly become clear, and practitioners will as a result be committed to achieving high standards in all aspects of practice.

Reflective practice questions

SUPPORTING CHILDREN'S PLAY

How do you encourage children to be active in their play and learning?

How do you identify additional resources to enhance play as part of continuous provision?

When do you stand back from children's play?

When do you join in with children's play?

How do you support children to take responsibility for developing their own play?

SUPPORTING CHILDREN'S LEARNING

Do you feel the children were absorbed and interested in the activity?

Can you identify what it was that helped children to be interested and involved in the experience?

Were children encouraged to take control and be actively involved in their learning during the activity?

How did you encourage children to be active in their play and learning?

SUPPORTING CHILDREN'S LEARNING

What do you feel the children learnt from the activity? How did it support their development?

Was this learning planned or spontaneous?

How could this learning be reinforced or built upon?

What types of resources were used and were there enough resources?

How did the children use the resources?

What further resources could have been used?

Were there any limitations to this activity?

Did the children extend the learning opportunity through the use of new resources or ideas?

The Self-Evaluation Form

Why is there now so much emphasis on the Self-Evaluation Form (SEF)? Research has proven that self-reflection and evaluation both support good practice within a setting as part of continual development. Importantly this self-reflection supports good outcomes for children.

The EPPE (Effective Provision of Pre-School Education) project was very influential in informing us of the significance of self-reflection and evaluation.

'The use of self evaluation...should enable settings to reflect on their current strengths and identify next steps which will have a direct impact on children's learning experiences.'

In their efforts to continually improve outcomes for children, Ofsted decided to implement a specific early years self-evaluation tool.

Although the completion of the Self-Evaluation Form is not compulsory, all settings are advised to complete the form. Both the completion of the form or the failure to complete the form can have a very significant effect on the outcome of your inspection.

- If you do complete your SEF, it is likely to decrease the length of the inspection and helps the inspector to know what to focus on in the inspection. If completed properly the SEF can ease the process of inspecting for the inspector.

- If you do not complete your SEF, you will more than likely be asked why and will need a good reason as to why it has not be completed.

- Failure to complete the form could also mean that your inspection will be longer and more searching. The self-evaluation criteria is likely to be graded lower, although the inspector will check to see what other methods of self-evaluation have been implemented.

Before tackling the SEF, it is worth spending some time reflecting on your setting and its current self-assessment strategies. Settings where reflective practice occurs regularly will find completion of the SEF a much easier task. For further tips on becoming a reflective practitioner please see the previous chapter.

Managers and leaders in settings need to consider what is already being done in the setting to evaluate quality and practice, and how good practice is shared throughout the setting.

The basic key questions of self-evaluation are:

- How are we doing?

- How do we know?

- What are we going to do now?

Involving all staff in the process of self-evaluation will produce higher standards and a sense of ownership over the process of continual development. It is worth remembering that self evaluation only works where individuals within a setting are committed to ensuring high standards and are able to look objectively at practice.

All practitioners need to be aware of what the priorities for improvement are as identified in the SEF, and their role in the ongoing process of working towards improvement. As the SEF is a working document which plays an important role in the development of the setting, please bear in mind that Ofsted will look to validate the statements in your SEF by questioning all staff, whether they are new-starters or not. It is essential then that the setting's SEF is included in the induction process so that all new members of staff are aware the setting's objectives.

Using reflective practice as part of your self-assessment process within the setting will greatly help and support completion of the Self-Evaluation Form. When you first look at the SEF it may look like a daunting task to complete it, but break it down section by section and setting yourself small completion steps can make it seem much more manageable.

The Self-Evaluation Form – what you need to know

Practicalities

- The SEF can be completed online and Ofsted recommend that you use this method.

- You can update your SEF online as often as you like, probably termly, but it should be updated no less than once a year.

- An annually updated hard copy needs to be sent to Ofsted.

- You need a copy of the SEF in the setting at all times ready for the inspector.

- To complete the online form you will need an Ofsted Security Token (OST), which is a unique password, and the guidelines on how to complete the online form. If you have not received an OST you need to contact Ofsted (08456 404043) quoting your Unique Reference Number (www.ofsted.gov.uk).

HINT: Around two days before your inspection, your online SEF will most likely be frozen. This will give you a warning that the inspector is on their way!

Tips for completing the SEF

- Start with the section you find easiest to complete to give yourself a boost, then progress gradually to completing all of the form.

- Make your statements clear and concise and add evidence to back up your statements e.g. refer to policies, planning, observations, records etc., and have these to hand for the inspector to review.

- Use bullet points rather than lengthy paragraphs.

- Try and convey as full a picture as possible of your setting.

- Use a dictionary if you're unsure of a correct spelling. To use a spell check you will need to cut and paste into a word document, as there is no spell check with the online form.

- Ensure you use appropriate terminology and language and avoid jargon and slang.

- Use the Ofsted guidance notes.

- Even though inclusion will be graded separately, it is important to reinforce it throughout the whole SEF.

How to grade yourself

- Be honest, if you feel your provision and/or practice in a specific area is outstanding say so and why.

- Even if you grade yourself as outstanding, you still need to identify areas for improvement and what you are hoping to do to make it even better.

- Ofsted will look at how their judgment compares to yours and in doing so will be evaluating your judgements and ability to self evaluate.

The self-evaluation form is broken down into three parts.

These parts are:

Part A

This part covers the setting details and views of those who use the setting. It details the characteristics of your setting and the background of the children. It also asks you to seek the views of all those who use your setting and how you use these views to improve the quality of the provision.

Part B

This covers the evaluation of the outcomes for children and should help you think about and assess your provision. You should answer the questions by taking account of the welfare, learning and development requirements and statutory guidance set out in the EYFS framework.

You should think carefully about any changes and improvements you have made since your most recent inspection. In the text boxes you should describe briefly what you think is working best and describe any plans you have to further improve provision.

Prepare to show Ofsted any evidence you have that supports what you are saying e.g. photographs, documents, risk assessment. These should then be available for the inspector when they visit.

RAG rating

The R in RAG stands for red, the A amber and the G green. This is a simply easily understood way of grading settings and being able to access the grading at a glance. The grading will of course be evidence based.

Most local authorities use a RAG rating to score how settings are doing. During inspection Ofsted may inquire about your RAG rating and it is advisable if you know it to record it on your SEF. The settings may be RAG rated at every visit or through annual dialogue or after an initiative involving the setting.

How the RAG rating works

Status	Definition	Action
RED	The setting is in need of support and is not meeting actions set by the local authority, or the statutory framework. The setting is at risk.	Greater support will be given by the local authority as a priority. The setting will be strongly encouraged to meet actions set within a strict timetable discussed with the setting. Together with the setting a quality improvement plan will be drawn up.
AMBER	The setting has one or two minor problems or a major problem that needs to be resolved before the local authority has the confidence to consider the setting Green.	The local authority will be aware of the problem and will sometimes send officers to support the setting to improve by writing a quality improvement plan with the setting. Actions will be within an agreed timeframe and the setting will be responsible for evidencing satisfactory improvement.
GREEN	There are no concerns about the setting. It is on target. If it is supported by officers of the local authority they are satisfied that actions are met in a timely manner to a high standard.	None, although the local authority will continue to monitor the setting and be available to give support when appropriate.

Preparing for inspection

As we reflect more and more on our practice, less and less specific preparation will be required for an Ofsted inspection as the idea is that 'we should always be ready'. When considering preparation for an Ofsted inspection we're not talking about the stereotypical image of the caretaker painting the walls two minutes before the inspector is due to arrive. In this chapter we are looking more broadly at what practitioners need to do to prepare for inspection, both physically and mentally, because readiness can't just be pulled out of the bag on the day. A knock on the door by the Ofsted inspector should be a welcome visit that isn't going to phase any of the practitioners in the setting because they are all prepared and equipped with the knowledge understanding and strategies to cope.

As previously mentioned, in preparation for inspection you need to ensure that your SEF is completed competently, accurately and that it is up to date. It isn't compulsory, but it is strongly recommended that you have it filled in. Not having done so could adversely effect the outcome of the inspection, so don't delay, guidance is given in this book to help you complete it. If you haven't completed the form before the inspection, you may be asked to do it on the day and this can cause anxiety and in the rush you could miss vital points, it simply isn't possible to fill it in properly under these conditions. Make sure that you have a hard copy on hand for yourself to refer to during the inspection.

As you update your SEF, be certain to send the updates to Ofsted – this is

easy to do online – so that they always have current and relevant information. The inspector will read your SEF before visiting your setting so (remember, the online version of the SEF may be frozen approximately two days before the inspection giving you clear indication that you are about to be inspected – but this is NOT a guarantee).

When starting the SEF you need to be organised and share the task of completing it between the entire staff team. Effective teamwork is an essential component in any setting. Without effective teamwork, a setting cannot function properly and maintain standards. The inspector will be very experienced in looking for and identifying signs that show teamwork is either effective or ineffective in the setting. The sense of teamwork in a setting reflects the culture and ethos. Leaders and managers in settings can use the following checklist to help gain an insight into the sense of teamwork established in different rooms and/or the setting as a whole.

Improvement

The Ofsted inspector will probably take points from the SEF to concentrate on during the visit – although this won't necessarily be the entire focus of the visit – but it does mean that information needs to be accurate and an honest reflection – this is no time for modesty! It is also a time to think of moving your practice forward in a positive way and

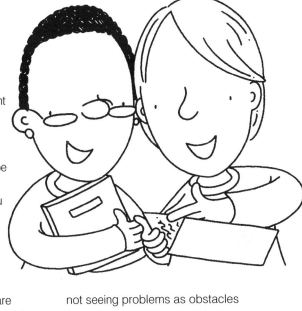

not seeing problems as obstacles or barriers to improvement but as challenges to overcome. But don't panic – nothing is perfect straight away and the inspector is not looking for perfection, but looking that you are moving forwards and trying to improve all the time. Even if you judge yourself to be outstanding she will want to see how you intend to improve even further. A positive outcome of having an accurately completed SEF could be that the inspector may not check out everything that you do and it may shorten the inspection. Not only do you need to complete your SEF but also get to know your SEF: be aware of, and have a working knowledge of, what actions are being taken, exactly what progress has been made, where your strengths are and where more work is required. It is important that the whole team is involved in this and not just the person responsible for completing the SEF.

If your setting is taking part in any kind of quality assurance award, it is useful to have the relevant information for that to hand also. Ofsted will be interested to see any completed or current modules with development plans and evidence of the impact these schemes have had on your practice and experiences for the children within the setting. If you have any certificates or plaques for quality assurance awards or training these need to be displayed, as they evidence continued professional development and good practice.

Now we need to think of the more practical things. Can the inspectors find your setting easily? Is the address and phone number up-to-date with Ofsted and are postcodes accurate for your building? This is especially important if the inspectors are using a satellite navigation system to find you.

If you are a pre-school or day care setting, are you clearly advertised and signposted? Are car parking places near by and easy to find? If the answer to these two questions is no, is there anything that you can do about it? There is nothing more stress-inducing than not being able to find your way somewhere, then not being able to park the car, not having the right change for the meter and then having a long walk laden down with bags – you really don't want your inspector to arrive to inspect you facing these sorts of conditions. It may be that all you can do is inform them before the visit where they will need to park and if they will need money and how much etc.

Consider the access to your building; this needs to be easy to use for all people including those with additional needs, such as a wheelchair. Can the inspector find where to get in? Is there an efficient way of the door being answered at all times including before the session begins?

Child-centred learning

With every action that you take, it is important to always ensure that the children are at the heart of all that

happens. You need to ask yourself how you put children at the centre of your practice and be able to demonstrate this to the inspector. So, for example if through peer observations you decided that your setting's welcome was poor and you decided to change it, you need to put the child at the heart and think 'what would make this a better experience for all the children?'. The next step is to involve the children and their parents and carers by asking for their opinions and valuing them, in this way they will then be far more supportive in implementing any change. Through peer observation you may realise that a particular member of staff does something especially well and may therefore decide to all use that method of practice throughout the setting.

At all times you need to ensure that your environment is safe and stimulating for children to learn and develop and to make any changes that are necessary. Use the skills you have learnt during reflective practice to assess this, asking yourself relevant questions such as: are there defined areas of learning? Is it bright and airy? Am I an effective practitioner, setting activities up in an inviting manner? Be aware that you need to have robust systems in place for risk assessments, equipment maintenance and safety checks.

It is vital to read through your last inspection as a whole team to address any outstanding issues and simply to remind yourselves of its content. Try not to take the previous report too personally or as criticism, if you can look at it more in terms of guidance for improvement you are more likely to have an open mind when making those improvements. Just because this is Ofsted it doesn't mean that the judgements are always accurate, so you need to consider them carefully and dispassionately and then act accordingly. It is vitally important that you have completed any actions from the previous Ofsted inspection. If you haven't then you need to be able to justify why this is the case.

When you look at the last report it is also a good time to reflect on all the improvements that you have made, however sometimes in the rush to improve certain areas it is easy to lose sight of the good you were already doing so this is a good time to make sure you haven't let some areas of good practice slide.

Your polices need to be always up-to-date, reviewed and in order. Best practice is to ensure that these are read and signed by each member of staff and committee members as proof that they have read them. It is also good to have enabled staff to contribute to policies in order to give them a sense of ownership. This can of course be a lengthy process, but you could consider one or two policies a month over the course of an academic year. Guidance on writing policies and the requirements of individual policies can be obtained from your local Early Years and Childcare Service or from the Pre-school Learning Alliance. Of course, all policies are important, but some details are more vital so pay particular attention that everyone is aware of the safeguarding children policy and those relating to staff conduct. It's also important that parents/carers are aware of policies and are able to access them – could you include a policy of the month on your newsletters for example to ensure staff and parents have a working knowledge of practice policies?

Be sure that your planning is up-to-date – it's good for it to be annotated with changes made in response to children, that's completely what the inspectors will want to see, but make sure this can be evidenced in your observations.

Talk to the staff – staff are likely to be anxious of inspections particularly if this is their first one or if they have had a bad experience of being inspected. It's best for staff to be prepared, so brief them with likely scenarios and empower them with responses. The inspector will speak to all staff members so it is important to help them to understand the way questions may be posed and the jargon that may be used. However, most important is to reassure staff of your faith in them and in their good practice so that they can relax and are able to perform to their best ability. This can be achieved through in-house training, constant communication via staff meetings, making sure all staff have access to and are supported during training so that they are well informed and knowledgeable on all aspects of their role.

Have you got an operational plan or a wish list? If so, consult it in preparation for inspection – are there any wishes that you could grant yourself? The feel-good factor of saying we've been able to develop our outdoor play recently by buying x, y or z is worth its weight in gold.

Are you part of a quality assurance scheme? Ofsted suggest that being part of such a scheme is not a guarantee of a good outcome but it is likely to have improved your practice in response to its questions and completed modules are helpful evidence for the inspector. It is estimated that somewhere in the

region of 85% of pre-school settings on a quality assurance scheme receive outstanding Ofsted judgements (www.ofsted.gov.uk).

Ofsted will consider your partnership with parents/carers – it is important that you do this too. Try to think of imaginative ways of sharing information with all parents/carers and enhancing your relationship with them so that they are not only informed but are able to become engaged in the setting – it is proven that parents/carers involved in this early stage of their child's education will be more likely to stay involved in later stages of their education.

Something that is often overlooked in preparation for an inspection is whether your setting is culturally aware, an excuse often proffered for not being is that 'we don't have any children from that culture here' – however it is even more important to reflect all members of a society for children who aren't going to have personal experiences of them so that they don't form prejudices and stereotypical viewpoints. Your inclusion practices are the golden thread that you will notice run through

all of the SEF questions, therefore it is something to consider extremely carefully and to be transparent about.

Continued professional development is a phrase on all of our minds. Make sure you are aware of all staff training needs and training already undertaken. For this you may need a training matrix which is included in this book. You will want to have a system in place whereby training is cascaded perhaps during staff meetings, or by a simple form that staff fill in when they have been on courses saying what they learnt and how it effected their practice – this can be displayed on the staff notice board for all to read, again a cascade form is included in this book.

This chapter links closely with the chapter on first impressions and it would be wise to go through that to make sure you have everything in place, we've talked a lot about implementing change, but be careful against making change for the just for the sake of it, if something is good and working well then leave it alone and give yourselves a pat on the back. It is just as important for the whole team to celebrate good practice and achievements as it is to be aware of areas in need of improvement.

On page 17 is an example form of how to record any training undertaken by staff, and on page 18 a suggested training matrix to track at a glance the qualifications and training of all staff.

How well the early years provision meets the needs of the range of children who attend

- Quality assessment, how well children are progressing from their starting points, evidence of regular summative assessment, taking into account how long a child has been in the setting and how often they

attend, this will include the 2-year-old progress check if applicable.

- Planning meets the needs of children and supports their own going development, is reflective, links to observation and is flexible and effective.

- There is consistency and quality in all practitioners obervations and assessment.

- Practitioner knowledge of the EYFS and the prime and specific areas of learning and development.

- Practitioners have high expectations for children and engage and enthuse.

- The setting engages with parents, sharing observations with them and welcoming their contributions.

- There are a variety of experiences for the children offering appropriate challenge.

The contribution of the early years provision to children's well-being

- Practitioners help children to form secure attachments and there is a key person system in place.

- There are strong relationships within the setting between practitioners as well as child to practitioner.

- The practitioners are effective role models.

- There are clear guidelines and strategies for behaviour, including promoting positive behaviour and managing challenging behaviour.

- All aspects of safety are considered, including the children feeling safe.

- The children are able to share concerns with practitioners.

- Healthy lifestyle promoted through diet and exercise.

- Children are encouraged to become independent.

- Children's physical needs are met.

- The environment indoors and outdoors is wel-resourced, stimulating, welcoming, and meets children's needs; including emotional needs.

- Transitions are supported, clear links between other settings.

- Care routines followed.

The effectiveness of leadership

- Responsibilities are fulfilled in relation to safeguarding and the welfare requirements.

- Clear understandings of the EYFS.

- Effective and rigorous systems of self-evaluation, with challenging targets set for improvement and the impact of any changes on the children tracked and recorded.

- Self-evaluation takes into account views of the children, staff and parents.

- Effective systems for supervision and appraisal of staff and their continuous professional development.

- Effective performance management systems.

- Training needs analysis for the setting and individual practitioners.

- Range of training completed and impact of training on improving children's well-being.

- Effective information sharing with others settings and professionals.

- Strong relationships with parents.

- Motivated and inspiring for staff.

- Effective sound systems for monitoring children's parents.

- Ensures policies and procedures are implemented and followed.

- Safe recruitment practices, induction and monitoring of new staff.

How well the early years provision meets the needs of the range of children who attend

OUTSTANDING – The provision is better than good because:

DESCRIPTOR	EVIDENCE	DEVELOPMENT
It consistently achieves very high standards across all aspects of its work with exceptional educational programmes for children of all ages. Practice is inspirational and worthy of dissemination to other providers.		
There are rich, varied and imaginative experiences for children delivered by practitioners who have very high expectations of themselves and the children, expert knowledge of the areas of learning, and a clear understanding of how children learn.		
Assessment at all ages is precise, sharply focused and includes all those involved in the child's learning. It is monitored and used to secure timely interventions and support, based on a comprehensive knowledge of the child and their family.		
Children are well motivated, very eager to join in and consistently demonstrate the characteristics of effective learning. The extremely sharp focus on helping them to acquire communication and language skills, and on supporting their physical, personal, social and emotional development helps all children make rapid improvement in their learning from their starting points with any gaps closing rapidly. They are exceptionally well prepared for school or the next steps in their learning.		
Highly successful strategies engage all parents in their children's learning in the setting and at home.		

The provision is good because:

DESCRIPTOR	EVIDENCE	DEVELOPMENT
The educational programmes have depth and breadth across the seven areas of learning. They provide interesting and challenging experiences that meet the needs of all children.		
The vast majority of practice is based on a secure knowledge and understanding of how to promote the learning and development of young children. Practice is consistently at least good and occasionally outstanding.		
All practitioners have high expectations of all children based on accurate assessment of children's prior skills, knowledge and understanding on entry to the setting. Practitioners complete regular and precise assessments of children and use these effectively to plan suitably challenging activities. They regularly listen perceptively to, carefully observe, and skilfully question children during activities in order to re-shape tasks and explanations to improve learning.		
Practitioners can demonstrate that all children, including those with special educational needs and/or disabilities and those learning English as an additional language, are progressing well towards the early learning goals over time, given their starting points. Children are interested and keen learners who display the characteristics of effective learning.		
Children are supported in the acquisition of communication and language skills and in their physical, personal, social and emotional development so that children of all ages and abilities make good progress in their learning. All children are generally working comfortably within the typical range of development expected for their age, taking account of any special educational needs and/or disabilities. Where children's starting points are below those of other children of their age, assessment shows they are improving consistently over a sustained period and the gap is closing. Children's progress in the prime areas of learning ensures they have the key skills needed for the next steps in their learning, including school where appropriate.		
The key person system supports engagement with all parents, including those who may be more reluctant to contribute. Parents contribute to initial assessments of children's starting points on entry and they are kept well informed about their children's progress. Parents are encouraged to support and share information about their children's learning and development at home. The key person system ensures all practitioners use effective, targeted strategies and interventions to support learning that match most children's individual needs.		

The contribution of the early years provision to children's well-being

OUTSTANDING – Care practitioners are better than good because:

DESCRIPTOR	EVIDENCE	DEVELOPMENT
All practitioners are highly skilled and sensitive in helping children form secure emotional attachments, and provide a strong base for their developing independence and exploration.		
Children increasingly show high levels of self-control during activities and confidence in social situations, and are developing an excellent understanding of how to manage risks and challenges relative to their age.		
All practitioners consistently give the highest priority to the safety of children and effectively support children's growing understanding of how to keep themselves safe and healthy.		
The strong skills of all key persons ensure all children are well prepared for the next stages in their learning. Practitioners skilfully support children's transitions both within the setting and to other settings and school.		
There is a highly stimulating environment with child-accessible resources that promote learning and challenge children both in and outdoors.		

The provision is good because:

DESCRIPTOR	EVIDENCE	DEVELOPMENT
A well-established key person system helps children form secure attachments and promotes their well-being and independence.		
Practitioners are good role models. They are deployed well, use consistently applied strategies and provide clear guidance for children about what is acceptable behaviour.		
Relationships are strong at all levels and children are learning to respect and tolerate each other's differences. Children are gaining an understanding of risk through activities that encourage them to explore their environment.		
Practitioners have a good understanding of and give a high priority to the safety of children. Children's behaviour shows that they feel safe in the setting. They are able to share concerns with their key person or other adults at the setting. Practitioners give clear messages to children to ensure they are developing a good understanding of why it is important to have a healthy diet and gain an understanding of the need for physical exercise.		
Practitioners help children to learn to be independent and encourage them to manage their own personal needs. Children are competent at managing their personal needs relative to their ages.		
There is a stimulating, well-resourced and welcoming environment, both in and outdoors, to support children's all-round development and emotional well-being, which provides a range of experiences that develop children's growing independence and cooperation.		
Children are well prepared for the next stage in their learning because practitioners provide appropriate support to prepare them for their transitions, both within the setting and to other settings and school.		

Cascade from training

Title of course attended	
Date of course attended	
Name(s) of staff attending the course	
General description of content of the course	
Three points for development from the course or ideas gained from the course	1. 2. 3.
On a scale of 1 to 10 how effective was the course in meeting your requirements (1 being lowest and 10 being highest) circle as appropriate then explain your answer.	1 2 3 4 5 6 7 8 9 10

Training matrix

Staff name	Qualification – Date gained	CRB – Date and number	First Aid – Date	Appraisal – Date	Supervision – Date	Safe guarding children – Date	Courses requested – identified at appraisal and supervision	Courses attended – Date	Cascade – yes/no – Date

'First impressions count'

The inspectors are professional people who aren't going to be fooled by the veneer of everything on the surface looking superficially good, but the practice being poor. They aren't going to make judgements solely based on their first impressions either, they are professionally far more objective than that.

However, the first impression does influence opinion and can change the feel of a visit. For example, the following statement is taken directly from an Ofsted report: 'It is obvious from the moment the doors open and the children rush in that this is a happy and lively place where learning is fun'.

Before they arrive, the inspector will have used their intuition to gauge what their expectations are and what they are going to find from reading your completed Self-Evaluation Form.

They will start by grading your setting as Good – it is up to you to prove otherwise. All their descriptors are for Good, if you do not meet this criteria then you are Satisfactory. If you exceed it you are Outstanding. The inspector will expect consistency – if the leadership and management are weak, the welfare of the children cannot realistically be good.

This chapter aims to explore first impressions and how we can ensure that they are favourable in getting a true reflection and judgement of your setting.

Arrival

Hopefully the Ofsted inspector will have arrived at your door safely,

having been informed and signposted of how to gain access to your building. On his/her walk from car or train to the door she is going to be looking around her to see if the setting is inviting and welcoming.

He/she is going to ring on your doorbell and may have to wait in the foyer for a few minutes, this can be an illuminating experience and one you should try yourself to give a true picture of what it is going to be like. Ask yourself the question: is the foyer warm, welcoming and comfortable? It's worth providing somewhere for parents and carers to sit. Does everyone in your foyer feel at ease and welcome?

Are any information and notices given in an accessible manner to everyone including those with additional needs?

My experience of standing waiting in the foyer, as a mother or as a visitor to a setting, have not always been a positive experience and can colour my view of that setting. As a visitor I often just stand and listen and wonder what it would be like to be a parent or child in that setting, especially a new parent – do I feel I belong? Or do I feel outside 'the group'? Are parents exchanging information which is sensitive and that really shouldn't be aired in public? Are they chatting about the setting in a positive and encouraging manner?

committee members who are present. Do show the inspector where he/she can put their bag and coat and where the toilets are. It is likely to be whoever is on the door that day that welcomes the Ofsted inspector so this could be the newest least trained member of staff. It is worth considering putting something in the staff induction programme of the setting that includes how to behave during Ofsted inspections – including some role play situations. If the inspector arrives at the start of the session when the door is busy how does the person on the door welcome them, manage to stay on the door and also inform the rest of the team that they are there? The solution to these types of problem will be different in every setting and need to be discussed during training days trying out various scenarios.

Try to ensure that the dynamics of your team remain always professional on inspection day. To witness the team working together in a friendly manner with good rapport will prove to the inspector that you work well together and will be supportive as a team during challenging times. Indicators of good team work are shared goals, respect and friendliness to one another. This is not about being matey it is about being professional and sincere in your approach to your work. The inspector will be experienced in what effective teamwork looks like below are some indicators of positive teamwork.

- Does the room appear organised?

- Are the staff communicating verbally, is their also evidence of non verbal communication e.g. message books?

- Are the children happy and on task and are their physical needs being met?

- Do the staff appear to be aware of their role and responsibilities?

- Is there a happy and positive atmosphere?

Am I spoken to or am I ignored? Is there something for me to do whilst I wait or something informative for me to read. The foyer is a hazy area of responsibility but you need to try and create an area that reflects the rest of the setting and shouldn't be overlooked in the whole picture.

It leaves a bad impression if the inspector has to ask for the book to sign in, so when they arrive please remember to show and ask them to sign in using the visitor's book. The visitor's book must have a column for the name, date, time in and out, company and purpose of visit. Also, don't forget to tell the inspector about your emergency procedures and if there are any emergency drills planned for that day.

Be sure to open up on time every day – if the inspector is waiting outside and you're late in opening the doors parents/carers may start to grumble it looks unprofessional and unorganised. (You may not receive brownie points for opening on time every day but you are sure to lose them for opening late!) This may mean that you need to consider

changing your practice to facilitate everything being ready and safe for the children to come in on time. If you have to put everything out each morning timing can be an issue – especially if your staff are made up largely of parents/carers who themselves need to drop children off at school. Can you think of ways to overcome this problem? If you have some staff who have no other commitments before sessions begin, they could be asked to come in a little earlier with the sole purpose of setting up – this needs to be transparent to all the staff or tension can build up within the staff team.

Greeting the inspector

The greeting – this can be a tricky one! You're about to be inspected – you're bound to be anxious and possibly more than a little tense – this is true for the whole team – but do try to relax, breath deeply, be friendly and above all be professional! Find the time please to introduce the inspector to the whole team, including any

- Are the displays up to date?

- Is a visual routine displayed?

- Do the children respond to the adults?

- Do the adults respond to the children?

Your approach to the children in the setting must also reflect normality – try to be the same with the children as you always are, any tension that you're feeling will rub off on them. It is so easy to detect false behaviour – the children will be the first to see through it!

You're not going to get an inadequate judgement if the day the inspector comes six children are crying, Johnie and Alice have just bitten each other, the school fish has died and a member of staff is emotional! Unless of course you leave the six children uncomforted, you don't help Johnie and Alice to resolve their dispute amicably, you leave the fish floating in the bowl and you let the member of staff wreak havoc! It's how you handle the situations you're faced with that count and also what caused them in the first place; could reflective practice have identified areas for improvement that would negate these problems? For example, have observations revealed that children are unsettled on arrival and have you and your team discussed ways to improve this situation, e.g. to move straight into free flow play at the beginning of a session?

It is important that all staff are identifiable, this is for children and parents and carers on an everyday level as well as for inspectors. You can achieve this simply and relatively cheaply by them all wearing name badges, or tabards or the same bright coloured tee-shirts. A named photograph, displayed with staff titles and responsibilities and also training is also a pleasant touch. Not only does being identifiable help everyone know who everyone else is it also demonstrates a sense of pride in your place of work.

Once the inspector has walked through the door, been greeted and signed in, he/she will no doubt pause and look around the room to get a feel for the place, to get an idea of the general ambiance, this is another chance to make a positive first impression. They will want to see a bright and airy clean room, that doesn't mean there is no paint or water or sand or glitter, those things are meant to be there. It means there aren't five-year-old cobwebs and displays of children's work that are so old that the paper is curled and the season has passed.

We all have our little foibles of what's important to us and the Ofsted inspector is no different there will be something that she is extra keen on to look at first, however during the course of the visit she will look at everything that she wants to. Some of the things that leave a lasting impression from first glance are listed on the check list in the book.

A good way to know what the first impression your setting may give is to try to experience it yourself, or visit other settings to see how their practice is similar or varies from yours and to identify your own strengths and weaknesses and see where improvements can be made. You could set up a video to record the beginning of your sessions or simply video around the setting – its amazing what you will see through this. Or get a fresh pair of eyes in to look for you, it worth asking your local early years team if they could evaluate some areas for you to provide reassurance. You should network with other local settings and within the team as you may get ideas that you could use. Peer observations with feedback and evaluation at staff meetings will help you to identify areas of strength both individually and as a team and identify those areas that require development – there is more information on these in the 'Preparing for your inspection' chapter of this book.

As mentioned at the beginning of this chapter, first impressions count – but they can be misguiding. I'm sure we've all formed impressions in the past only to be proven wrong. So it doesn't all hang on first impressions, it's more about good practice which will become evident during the visit. However, if things start off badly and the view is tainted, it can prove to be a long haul to get things back on track.

First impressions checklist

What the inspector may look for	Comment	Met	Partly Met	Not Met
Is there a range and variety of activities available that are age/stage appropriate?	Are you sure that activities suit all children in the setting – e.g. no small parts?			
Are activities set out on different levels?	Are there table top, floor, wall activities?			
Do activities encourage exploration and investigation?	Do adults model investigation and exploration?			
Are resources up to date and relevant?	Children need to experience activities relevant to their lives.			
Are all resources fit for purpose?	All pieces present for puzzles, no splinters on wood, all pages of books.			
Is the children's paint fresh?	Is paint stirred and refreshed daily – are there plenty of colours for children to mix?			
Is the playdough fresh?	Do the children make the playdough themselves, is there a choice of colour, texture and tools etc?			
Can children initiate their own play through free choice?	This will be apparent immediately.			
Are resources clearly labelled with words and pictures?	Children first learn to read through looking at pictures and identifying symbols and making representations.			
Are all the staff interacting and engaging with the children?	This can include observing the children.			
Is there a clear learning intention to each activity?	Would every adult present know what you are hoping to get from each activity?			
Are the activities provided exciting?	Ask yourself 'Would I want to play here if I was a child?'.			
Do the children appear to be happy and engaged?	If children are bored they can become frustrated.			
Do children and adults appear to have a sense of pride in this setting?				
Are there displays of children's work? Are these clearly labelled, perhaps with a child's photo?	Is every child's work included? Are these up to date? Is all the work displayed the children's own or is it done by adults?			
Are displays child height?	Are they bright and colourful?			
Would all children feel that they belong here?	Does each child have their own peg, tray etc?			
Are staff easily identifiable?	Do the staff wear uniforms or name badges?			
If English was not my first language could I access information?	Consider how you make sure that messages are received and understood?			
Is there a visual timetable?	This helps children with routine and transitions.			
Is there access to plenty of malleable materials?	There should be around five malleable activities available in a pre-school setting.			
Do children know who their key person is?	Have you got key person lists with photographs of the key persons?			
Are areas of learning easily identifiable?	Do children and adults know where to go to do each activity?			
Does the setting smell fresh?	This is especially important in settings used by others and if there are stale food smells.			

What the inspector may look for	Comment	Met	Partly Met	Not Met
Do children have free access to drinking water?	This is better free flowing water but be sure it's fresh daily.			
Are the toilets well stocked with soap, handtowels and toilet paper etc.?	It is best practice to use sqeezie bottle soap not bars of soap.			
Is there access to natural materials?	Its good to have natural resources indoors and outdoors.			
Are all cultures equally reflected amongst toys, displays etc.?	This is especially important where some cultures are not physically present.			
Is there free flow play indoors and outdoors?	Are staff actively encouraging free flow?			
Are all staff well deployed?	Does every member of staff know what they are doing and why they are doing it?			
Is statutory paperwork displayed? Where?	E.g. Insurance certificate, Ofsted registration etc.			
Is there any evidence of a Quality improvement plan?	Do you have a quality improvement plan that you can show the inspector – perhaps you are part of a quality improvement award scheme.			
Would I know what to do in case of emergency in this setting?	Remember to tell every visitor your emergency plan when they arrive.			
Are first aiders identified?	Is there a notice displayed with first aiders names?			
Is there clear evidence of a strong partnership with parents/carers?	This will be evident in parent rotas, the rapport between parents and staff etc.			
Is the building secure?	Make sure any gates etc. are locked.			
Are you taking part in any initiatives, for example Unicef Rights of respecting children award	Make sure Ofsted are aware of any involvement and commitment with other organisations.			

Step-by-step guide to completing your Self-Evaluation Form

Part A: Section 1 – Your setting

This is the only section of the SEF that Ofsted can quote verbatim in the report – be sure it is factual and to the point.

You need to state the number of children who use the setting and give a brief description of their ages, genders, social and cultural backgrounds and whether they have learning difficulties and special educational needs.

Here you can list any special features of your setting e.g. participation in a quality assurance scheme.

Questions from Ofsted SEF guidance page 5	Features to consider
Your building including area and rooms used.	Describe your building – its age and style. List any other users.
The area your provision is in.	Is it a residential or industrial area, rural or urban?
Any access to an outdoor space.	Do you have an outdoor area that children can use on a daily free flow basis? If not what access to outdoor play do you have?
Access to and within the building – such as a lift ramp or stairs.	Describe access and give consideration to access for those with additional needs. This must include plans for what you would do should a need arise.
The days and hours you operate.	
The number and qualifications of the adults working with the children and any support staff, such as a cook.	List the qualifications of all staff – check with current legislation that levels and percentages are correct.
Recent training attended or any qualifications gained.	List training taken within the past year including any relevant short courses.
Difficulties in recruiting and retaining staff.	Describe any problems you may have had in this area.
Recent or impending re-organisation or change of staff.	Is anyone about to leave or to become qualified? Is there any impending internal promotion?

Part A: Section 2 – Views of those who use your setting

Questions from Ofsted SEF guidance page 6	Features to consider/ reflective questions	Evidence suggestions
How do you know what their views are? Do you ask parents/carers and others to complete a questionnaire about how satisfied they are with the provision or do you meet with parents/carers to discuss the provision?	Did you issue a questionnaire to ask parents/carers their views? Are parents/carers given an open door access to the setting and an opportunity to air their views? Do you have a questionnaire for new parents/carers as part of the settling-in process? Do you give out the questionnaire annually and an exit questionnaire?	How did you use the information gained from responses to questionnaire? Have you got examples of changes made as a result? Do you have a summary sheet of key responses? Do you have evidence of dates and times of such meetings and copies of questionnaires? Do you have a summary of responses to questionnaires?
Are parents/carers represented on the management body?	Parents/carers group/pre-school committee.	
How do you know children's views and ideas and those of the staff?	Do you do a review of each session with the children? Do you regularly ask children for their views and ideas of what they would like to do with the provision? Are staff able to express their ideas freely and are these ideas embraced if practically possible? Do you have staff interviews and appraisals to consider their views and ideas?	Children could be given cameras and asked to take photographs of areas they like or dislike about the setting – e.g. outdoor space. What changes have you made in response to those views – show evidence e.g. in the form of an action plan.

Part B: The quality and standards of the Early Years provision

The table below will help you to consider the questions on page 7 and 8 of the SEF guidance booklet.

Links can be made to EYFS card 4.4 Areas of Learning and Development and EYFS pages 4 – 12 'Development Matters'. You must be able to show academic progress.

Section 3: How well the early years provision meets the needs of the range of children who attend

Questions from pages 7 and 8 – Ofsted SEF guidance	Features to consider	Evidence suggestions
How do you promote children's learning and development? What is your overall approach to the children's learning and development?	Is your planning child-centred? Are children able to make choices? Can children lead activities? What is the proportion of child-initiated and adult led activities?	Copies of plans annotated with responses to children's interests, link this to observations. Choices must go beyond the choice of whether to participate in an activity or not.
How do you meet the needs of each child who attends your provision?	Do you have a system of observing and for evaluating observations of every child? Do you have robust partnerships with parents to identify needs and interests of their children? Do staff attentive listen to children recognising their needs and interests?	Copies of observations using a variety of observation methods detailing every child's individual learning journey. Do you record evidence of the voice of the parent and child? Examples could be displayed as parent's voice with ideas alongside reflecting that voice.
How do you know that children are making progress towards the early learning goals and enjoying learning?	How do you ensure that all areas of learning are accessed by each child including the outdoor environment? Do you make regularly observations in all areas of learning? Is there a strategy to ensure you are working towards goals using the development matters descriptors as a guide? Is there evidence of a balance of adult led and child initiated activities? Do you have sufficiently high expectations of children and what methods do you use to motivate them. Do you establish starting points for each child with assessment.	Copies of observations indicating what next steps are required for the child – these need to be carried forward to note when next steps are tried and the results. Evidence of motivational activities which will excite children and encourage them to learn. Recorded starting points for each child in their profile.

How well do you and any assistants of staff who work with you do the following:

Questions from pages 7 and 8 – Ofsted SEF guidance	Features to consider	Evidence suggestions
Plan the learning environment that supports children's play and exploration in and out of doors.	Do you adjust continuous provision to reflect individual needs? Do you plan the indoor and outdoor environment in a way that children can access all areas of learning – are areas of learning clearly defined? Are all areas of learning covered each session both indoors and outdoors?	Use plans of resources and activities provided with photographic evidence.
Is there a balance of adult-led and child-led activities that helps children to think critically and be active and creative learners.	Do children have choice? Do you allow uninterrupted free flow play? Do you use open-ended resources? How do you demonstrate to children that the end product may not always be important? How do you support children in making connections between experiences?	Open-ended resources are those that have no specific purposes e.g. boxes, leaves, lengths of material, these things and others allow critical thinking and problem solving.
Plan for individual children to ensure that they achieve as much as they can. This needs to take into account their culture and background including children with special educational needs and those children who achieve beyond expectations.	Do you have an inclusion officer? Does your inclusion officer attend all relevant meetings and training and then cascade information? Do you meet the needs of all children including different learning styles? How do you ensure continuity of care? Do you liaise with outside agencies? Do you have a gifted and talented scheme and are you able to encourage children who achieve beyond expectations to progress further?	
Use information from observation and assessment to plan personalised support for every child to ensure that children achieve as much as they can.	This is about using the planning cycle, refer to previous answer.	
Support each child in their learning and work with parents and carers as partners in children's learning and development.	How do you involve parents in the work of the setting? Do you have parent consultation meetings at a time and place convenient to parents and carers? Do parents contribute to policies, observations and children's records.	Research shows that if parents are engaged in early years provision they will remain so throughout their child's education – however we must respect that some parents do not want to be so involved. What do you do to embrace all parents e.g. home visits, translating documents and letter. Do you have a policy of the month for parents and staff to comment on – show examples of changes made in response to this. Do you include parents observations of their children in the children's records.

Part B: Section 3 continued

How well do you and any assistants of staff who work with you do the following:

Questions from pages 7 and 8 – Ofsted SEF guidance	Features to consider	Evidence suggestions
Offer an inclusive and welcoming service to all children.	Refer to questions on card 2.2 EYFS – Do you display lists from home languages? Find out from parents greetings that they use – encourage parents and staff to use these greetings. Make sure that everyone parent, carer, sibling etc receives a warm welcome. Find out about dietary needs of children. Welcome parents and carers into the care room. Value parents observations of their children.	Consider your welcome routine – could this be improved? Does the key person welcome all of their key children? Remember that this also includes individual needs and learning styles. Make sure you reflect positive images. On observation and consultation proformas have spaces for parents comments.

Section 4 – The contribution of the early years provision to children's well-being

You may find it helpful to refer to development matters to help you to answer these questions. These questions are about the emotional environment and how you ensure that children feel secure and how you ensure that they are physically healthy and well cared for.

Questions from page 8 Ofsted SEF guidance	Features to consider	Evidence suggestions
How well do children form appropriate bonds and secure emotional attachments with their carers?	Do you have a key person system with someone to cover should that key person not be available? Do the children know who their key person is? Does the key person keep records of children confidential? Does the key person have responsibility for the care routines of their key children? Do children spend the majority of time with their key carer?	Are there photos of key people and lists of their children? Do key people greet their children and spend time with them each session and form a special relationship with carers of their key children and liaise with other providers. Does the key person feed the child and change nappies etc. Do you have a mother duck system where the key carer is with their children most of the time throughout each session?
How effectively you encourage children to learn to behave well and develop good relationships with their peers. Do you: ■ Develop the habits and behaviour appropriate to good learners, their own needs and the needs of others ■ Join in make friends respect each other and take account of each other's diverse needs and backgrounds ■ Respond to the expectations of others ■ Make choices and decisions.	Do you create an atmosphere and an environment where children will want to learn and be able to engage and concentrate? Do you provide activities that arouse curiosity and anticipation? Are children encouraged by good example to value what others say – e.g. being quiet whilst others are speaking. Are you positive and good role models – are adults within the team friendly towards each other? Do you use discussion, puppets and story time to help children understand the qualities of friendship and do you encourage the language of friendship? Do you help children resolve their differences with empathy and sensitivity? Can children sometimes choose who they sit next to e.g. for snack or lunch time?	Open-ended resources are those that have no specific purposes e.g. boxes, leaves, lengths of material, these things and others allow critical thinking and problem solving.
Develop the characteristics of effective learning.	Refer to the characteristics of effective learning in the revised EYFS. Do practitioners encourage children to explore their surroundings and use their imagination?	Evidence of activities that are exciting which will encourage children to explore.

Section 4 continued

Questions from page 8 Ofsted SEF guidance	Features to consider	Evidence suggestions
Practice helping children to develop an understanding of the importance of physical exercise and a healthy diet.	Consent from parents to transport their children to hospital in case of emergency? What is your medicine policy? What hygiene routines do you have? Do you talk to children about the spread of infection and how to reduce this? You should have up to date information from parents or carers of child's medical conditions, allergies, special diet etc. How well you teach children to: ■ Be active and understand the benefits of physical activity? ■ Understand and adopt healthy habits? ■ Make healthy choices about what to eat and drink?	Copy of policy. Copy of healthy eating policy. This is about more than only having fruit at snack time it is about giving children healthy options and informed choices for a balanced diet and including foods from other cultures. Menu. Pictorial instructions for hand washing and nose blowing etc. Copy of food hygiene certificates. Named person responsible for health and safety.
How do you prepare children for transitions?	Do you have school visits? Do you talk to children about transitions? Are you prepared to support children in of times of bereavement and distress. e.g. parental separation? Do key carers support children's transition? Do staff from next class/school visit children in the setting? Do you have home visits?	School uniform in dress up area. Books and contacts to support children in times of emotional trauma. Care cards. Photos of family and friends displayed.

Section 5 – The leadership and management of the early years provision

You may not have in place all these recommendations, but do mention those that you have implemented, the positive effect they have and those you intend to implement soon. You may need to refer to the safeguarding and welfare requirements. If you are a child minder you need to consider how well you work with others and how you network.

Questions from page 9 Ofsted SEF guidance	Features to consider/ reflective practice	Evidence suggestions
How well do you consider your responsibilities in meeting the learning and development and safe guarding and welfare requirements of the EYFS?	Firstly, do you know what your responsibilities are – have you read and understood and have a working knowledge of the statutory framework of the EYFS? Do you access support where needed? Do you ensure that all staff are aware of requirements and have working knowledge of your policies and procedures? Are staff included in te drafting of policies and procedures?	Copies of the EYFS. Policies and procedures that reflect the EYFS requirements. Do you cascade policies and procedures? Do you access training?
Oversee the educational programmes to ensure that all areas of learning are included, assessment is consistent and used well to inform planning.	Are you aware of all the areas of learning and the aspects within them – do you oversee the environment to ensure that continuous provision reflects all areas of learning both inside and outdoors? Is there an approach to observation and panning that ensures all staff are consistent – are staff fully aware of all procedures of observation and planning and how these support child development. Is each member of staff aware of the stage each child is at, their learning styles and their next steps? Do you as leader have overall knowledge of these aspects to support staff?	The planning and observation cycle used by all members of staff to progress children. This should not be too onerous or paperwork heavy and should be able to be managed by all staff. An environment that reflects all areas of learning.
Promote equality and diversity and have a clear overview of the progress of all children who attend.	As above. Do you ensure that all adults and children are included and that unacceptable behaviour and attitudes are challenged? Do all areas promote inclusion – for example are there books reflecting disability, age, gender etc?	Equality of opportunity policy. Unicef rights of respecting children award. Well-resourced book area. Dolls of various ethnicity. Welcome in several languages. Staff reflecting cultures of children in the setting.

Questions from page 9 Ofsted SEF guidance	Features to consider/ reflective practice	Evidence suggestions
Work in partnership with parents and others.	Is there an open door policy whereby parents can easily approach staff?	A witness statement from a parent/carer.
	Do you have a policy and procedure to support parents with transitions of their children?	'All About Me' forms.
		Parental/carer observations.
	Are 'All About Me' forms completed with key person, parents and children?	Parental/carer contributions to two year progress check.
	Are parents made aware of your policies and procedures? If so how? Do parents have the opportunity to be involved in the writing of policies?	Photographs.
		Dates and times of consultation meetings.
		Parents' or carers' comments about consultations.
	How do you liaise with other providers, other professionals who may work with a child and schools to ease transitions and inform parents? Do you have regular consultation meetings?	Copy of diaries.
		Witness statement from parents/carers.
	Do you complete daily or weekly home setting diaries?	Photographs.
		MP3 recordings.
	Do you give parents free access to observations on their children?	Copies of newsletters.
	Are you welcoming, accommodating and friendly to parents when they enquire about their children's progress?	
	Do you regularly take photographs of children?	
	Do you record children's development for language on an MP3 player or similar and compare to later development to share with parents? Do you give parents ideas on how to extend activities and interests at home that have begun in the setting?	
	Do you hold workshops for parents and carers to understand child development?	
	Do you explain to parents/carers the stage of development a child is at?	
	Do you enable children to have schemas and support parents in understanding these?	
	Do you hold functions such as sports day etc at times when people are likely to be able to attend – e.g. those who work?	
	Do you make home visits to parents/ carers who find it difficult to get to the setting?	
	Do you use parents as working parties?	
	Do you give parents ideas on how to extend activities and interests at home that have begun in the setting?	

Questions from page 9 Ofsted SEF guidance	Features to consider/ reflective practice	Evidence suggestions
Work in partnership with parents/carers/ guardians and others continued.	Do you hold workshops for parents and carers to understand child development? Do you explain to parents/carers the stage of development a child is at? Do you enable children to have schemas and support parents in understanding these? Do you hold functions such as sports day etc at times when people are likely to be able to attend – e.g. those who work?	
How well do you evaluate your provision?	Have you indentified any weakness and set targets for improvement – do you have a quality improvement plan? Are you working with the local authority or others to improve?	Quality improvement plan stating the expected benefits of improvement and a time frame to improve with small actions that are achievable.
How well do you safeguard children?	It is a recommendation that the Criminal Records Bureau (CRB) check is reviewed every three years – staff have a duty to inform leadership of anything that may affect their CRB rating. Are all staff CRB checked? Have all staff been on a safeguarding course within the last three years? Do you explain safety rules to children in a way which they can understand and involve them in drawing up a contract of ground rules? Do you practice safety routines regularly recording and evaluating their outcomes? Do you have effective systems to ensure that ratios are kept at all times not only throughout the setting but in individual rooms Do you ensure that all equipment is safe and regularly check this? Do you evaluate your accident and incident book to consider if there are improvements that you can make to lessen these? Do you build up good relationships with parents and carers so that concerns can be addressed from a stand point of mutual trust? Do all staff and parents and children realise that they have a responsibility to report issues of concern regarding safety?	Evaluation of safety check forms. Copy of health and safety policy. Ground rule contract. Copy of CRB Forms. Training matrix.

Questions from page 9 Ofsted SEF guidance	Features to consider/ reflective practice	Evidence suggestions
How well do you safeguard children? continued.	Is your provision used for your sole use during session time? Do you have a named officer responsible for health and safety?	
How well do you ensure the suitability and qualifications of all adults looking after children or having unsupervised access to them?	Do you take up references of all candidates for vacancies? Do you plan and record continued professional development for all staff according to need? Do you look at certificates to validate claims of qualifications? Do you liaise with tutors of qualification courses to see how staff are doing? Do you support staff when they cascade information and ideas from courses?	Copies of advertisements for vacancies. Record of success.
How well do you maintain all records that are required for safe and efficient management of the setting and to meet all children's needs?	Where do you keep records? How do you ensure confidentiality and who has access to records? When do you record? How do you ensure data protection on records kept on computers and outside the setting?	Copy of data protection details. It is important to make sure that records are kept on site or at least are always there when the setting is running unless you have a prior arrangement with Ofsted. You need to check with Ofsted the records that need to be kept on site.
The effectiveness of your policies and procedures including your complaints procedures.	Do you review policies regularly allowing parents and staff to contribute in the review? Do you have many complaints? If not is this an indication that things are working well or are people too afraid to comment!?	Copy of policies. Give examples of changes made to policies as a results of review.
How well do you ensure the suitability and safety of outdoor and indoor spaces furniture equipment and toys?	Do you take out annual risk assessments and daily safety checks? Do you buy appropriate equipment which is quality assured and have available suitable equipment for the age/stage of development of children using it? Do you have someone responsible for maintenance of equipment?	Copies of daily safety checks with actions taken.
The quality and effectiveness of risk assessments and actions you take to manage or eliminate risks.	Do you analyse incidents and accidents to see if there are adjustments that can be made to lessen the likelihood of accidents happening? Reviewing risk assessments.	Record of accident books and incident books with records of actions taken to ensure less risk in the future. Copy of risk assessment forms and daily safety checks with adjustments made as a result of these.

Questions from page 9 Ofsted SEF guidance	Features to consider/ reflective practice	Evidence suggestions
The effectiveness of the steps you take to promote children's good health and well being including those to prevent the spread of infection and those taken when children are ill.	In your routine do you allow time for rest? Does your routine allow time for physical exercise for all children? Do you have posters etc. showing children's routines, such as hand washing or nose blowing? How do you prevent the spread of illness –and care for children who become ill whilst with you? Do you have a named first aider? Is the first aid kit is well stocked and checked regularly? This needs to be signed. Do you use gloves when administering first aid? Do you wear coloured plasters on cuts when preparing food? Do parents know that they are responsible for keeping you informed of their children's health issues – e.g. contact with infectious disease? Do you have a protocol of informing parents when there is an outbreak of infectious disease? What do you do if a child tells you on arrival that they have been sick during the night? Does your policy state that in case of sickness a child should not return for at least 48 hours? Do you sterilise all feeding equipment and resources? Do you update children's medical history regularly? Do you have spare clothing? Do you dispose of nappies etc. appropriately? Do you ensure that any animals kept on the premises or visiting the premises do not pose a health risk? Does your setting have good ventilation?	Copies of routine showing time allowed for rest and exercise. Copies of routine posters. Witness statement from staff demonstrating support. Notices. Newsletters. Training log. First aid kit – with stock list signed and dated. Prospectus with information relating to keeping healthy.
How well do you work in partnership with parents/carers and others to safeguard children?	Do you offer informative advice to parents/carers with children with infectious illnesses? How do you consult with parents/carers about issues relating to child protection?	Copies of notes to parents/carers.

Section 5 – The leadership and management of the early years provision continued

Questions from page 9 Ofsted SEF guidance	Features to consider/ reflective practice	Evidence suggestions
How well do you work in partnership with parents/carers and others to safeguard children?	How do you keep parents/carers informed? Do staff have a working knowledge of what everyone needs to do? Are records kept securely, confidentially and accurately?	
The staff's knowledge and understanding of child protection/ safeguarding issues and procedures.	Do you address the issue of safe guarding children procedures in your staff induction procedures? Are staff sent on training?	Certificates from staff safe guarding children training. Copy of induction procedure. Copy of 'What to do if you suspect a child is being abused'.
The extent to which any recommendations and actions raised at the previous inspection have been tackled in terms of improved outcomes for children.	Do you have an action plan from the last inspection? Have you exceeded the action plan if so how?	Explain how the action plan worked, any difficulties and barriers that you encountered and how these were overcome.
Any improvements you have made to promote the equality and inclusion that have had a beneficial impact on all children.	This needs to include specific examples e.g. have you purchased any equipment or books that support inclusion?	Photographs. Written evidence – e.g. letter from parents.
The extent to which improvements have had a positive impact on the overall quality of the service you provide and the outcomes for children.	Describe the positive impact of change. Did you have SMART targets?	

The EYFS Inspection in practice

Section 6 – The overall quality and standards of the early years provision

Put everything together from previous questions and demonstrate to Ofsted how good your setting is.

Refer to guidance notes page 10 for this section. You are justifying the

judgements you have made in the three key areas – use the Evaluation Schedule as a help.

Overall quality – what you need to consider	Features to consider/ reflective practice	Evidence suggestions
The progress all children make in their learning and development relative to the starting points and their readiness for the next stage of their education.	You will need to have the starting points for all children. These need to be true starting points not points after the child has settled because this may help identify needs for their next transition. You will need to show evidence of progress for all children and how you can ensure this.	Children's profile including starting points and next steps.
The extent to which your practice meets the needs of all children who attend including nay children who may be disadvantaged or need additional support because of their home or background or any Special Educational Needs.	You will need to prove a thorough knowledge of all children and their backgrounds and needs so that none can slip through the net – this will require a good partnership with parents and other professionals.	
Children's personal and emotional development including whether they feel safe and secure and happy.	You will need to refer to the characteristics of effective learning on pages 6 and 7 of the EYFS and consider how your provision supports this.	Witness statements from parents attesting to the happiness of their children. Photographs.
Whether the requirements for children's safeguarding and welfare are met.	Using the safeguarding and welfare requirements check that all are met.	
Your effectiveness in evaluation practice and securing continuous improvement that improves your provision.	Ofsted will check how you evaluate your provision and how you grade yourself – it is important to be honest here – if you feel you are outstanding and can justify this then grade yourself as outstanding do not be modest and record a good grading as this could lead Ofsted to the opinion that you are not recognising outstanding practice when you see it.	Quality improvement plans. Quality improvement awards. Training. Using parents and children to reflect on provision and noting their views.

The inspection day

What the inspector may do before the inspection

- Check which register the provider is on.

- Check the accuracy of the information about individuals connected with the inspection.

- Review any information where there is a concern.

- Consider the previous report if there is one and note any points to follow up.

- Check whether any information has been received since the date of registration or the last inspection.

- Review the provider's self-evaluation where available.

- Check whether the providers have a webpage, as this may give useful information.

- Draft a brief note about lines of inspection enquiry.

So the inspector has arrived, what should you do? The most important thing is to carry on as normal, once you've got over the first feelings of 'they're here'! Carrying on and treating it as a normal day ensures stability for the children and that you will be showing yourselves at your best to the inspector. What you don't want is the inspector to hear a member of staff saying to you or someone else "why are you doing that?", implying that what is happening is not normal practice.

Be as accommodating as possible, remember the inspector will have a laptop with them to record their observations and findings, and therefore will need space in each room. It is probably worth mentioning at this point that the inspector is not there to look for negatives, but will be looking to see how you demonstrate that the Early Years Foundation Stage (EYFS) is in practice in your setting.

Your staff team will need support and may well be feeling particularly nervous. It is important they feel reassured, particularly after being asked questions by the inspector.

How to support your staff team during an inspection:

You'll know your team, so you'll know who will be unfazed by the inspector arriving and who might be nervous.

To alleviate the panicking you just need to carry on as normal and give reassurance as necessary.

Introduce members of staff confidently to the inspector and mention their role in the setting and the level of qualification, as well as their name.

Also make sure that the kettle is always ready to boil, there are plenty of clean mugs and milk ready for staff during their breaks!

What about if you have doubts about your inspector?

Your doubts might be about general awareness, competency, conduct and level of professionalism.

It is very unlikely that this would happen, but there are few steps to follow if this should occur.

Talk to another senior member of staff to see if they have doubts as well.

If you feel you do have cause for concern and that the inspection judgment might be compromised, you should talk to the inspector, so the situation can hopefully be resolved there and then. If you are not happy with the outcome of this conversation, you should phone Ofsted on 08456 404040. Formal complaints can be made at any stage during the inspection or up to thirty calendar days from the date of publication of any report.

Feedback

So, the inspection is over and you're about to receive your feedback from the inspection. Take a couple of deep breaths and remember the following:

- Make sure you go somewhere quiet for the feedback, and ensure staff know not to interrupt you.

- Listen carefully.

- Jot down key points.

- Ask questions to help your understanding and to clarify points.

- If you're unclear about something ask for specific examples to help understanding.

- Acknowledge the feedback.

- Try not to focus just on any negatives but remember the positives as well and see the negatives as points for developing and improving practice.

- Take time to sort out in your head what has been said before feeding back to the rest of the staff team.

Remember feedback is two-way and if you feel you have justification to challenge something that has been said, then do so clearly, concisely and with evidence which can be verbally explained. Then you still will feel confident about it after the inspector has gone.

Unless the outcome of the inspection was inadequate or you have been given a time limit on certain points for action, give yourself a few days grace to digest all that has been said. Having given yourself this time, you will then be in a better position to take action on the points raised and identifying how to move forward and improve with your practice.

Meeting between the inspector and the provider

As part of the inspection, the inspector will want to meet with the provider or manager. It will be at a convenient time for the setting, usually near the start of the inspection, so anything discussed can be followed up.

In a childminding setting or a group setting operating from one room e.g. a pre-school in a village hall, the meeting will most likely take place when the children are engaged and when appropriate during the general observations of the setting. Obviously, the inspector will recognise that you will still have to supervise the children and meet their needs. In a setting where the provider/manager is supernumerary and the meeting takes place in another room or office, the meeting should take no longer than an hour and will probably be much shorter.

If the manager or nominated person has changed since the last inspection, the inspector will need to ensure that the provider meets the requirements of the EYFS. The inspector will need to establish that roles and responsibilities are clear for the manager and/or provider, this will include the provider's legal accountability.

The initial discussion will refer to issues being followed up during the inspection and times should be agreed for further discussion, so that the inspector can feedback to the provider.

The inspector will evaluate the following:

- Whether the leaders' and managers' roles are clearly established and whether they meet and understand the requirements of the EYFS.

- How well the planning, assessment and delivery of the areas of learning and development are monitored and the extent to which children's needs are identified and met through appropriate intervention.

- The effectiveness of staff supervision, appraisal, performance management, training and ongoing professional development.

- How self evaluation is used in identifying and informing priorities and setting challenging targets for improvement. This will include how the views of parents, children and any partners contribute to self evaluation and progress towards any actions raised at the last inspection or monitoring visit.

- The consistency of practice and how standards are set and maintained.

- How effective the setting is in working with other professionals and partnership work needed to support children with identified needs.

- Safeguarding policies, procedures and effectiveness, including child protection procedures, risk assessments, staff recruitment procedures and staff supervision.

The variety of observations the inspector may use during the inspection

- Observation of a specific activity or age group for around 20 to 30 minutes. This will enable the inspector to see several practitioners

and help them to gauge whether the seven areas of learning and development are all reflected in what is on offer to the children. They will also be able to see how children of different ages/ stages of development/abilities are supported. For pre-school aged three and four children, the inspector will observe how their literacy skills are developing and how ready the older children are for school.

- Tracking a small group of children to assess their experiences (see opposite).

- Longer observations, over 30 minutes, this is particularly relevant in baby rooms, where it may be necessary in order to observe care routines, attachments and activities. This type of observation may also be used to capture best practice or to get a clearer insight into weaker practice to provide evidence to support recommendations.

- Short observations of several activities, this is often used when the children are in one room and move around the activities depending on their interests.

Joint observations: the inspector and provider observing together

In group settings the inspector will invite the provider or a nominated senior member of staff to join them in one or more observations of activities, care routines and/or scrutiny of children's progress. It is entirely up to the provider whether or not they wish to participate. There are pros and cons

Ofsted feel that joint observations help them to:

- Get clear understanding of the provider's accuracy and skills in monitoring and evaluation

of practice and professional development programme for practitioners.

Ofsted also feel it gives the provider an opportunity to contribute to the evidence used to make judgements about the provision.

Points to consider and remember

- You and the inspector need to agree what is to be observed.

- After the observation, they should discuss their views of what has been seen in relation to the quality of the practice. The inspector will expect the provider/manager to give their views first considering the strengths, what went well and what could have made it better and a general summation.

- If the practice observed is weak, the inspector will ask you the provider/manager what action you are taking if any or what action you will take to improve the practice. The inspector will discuss with you when and how to feedback to the practitioner, the inspector may wish to observe your feedback.

- If you write your observation, the inspector must look at this and any differences explored. Note you make will not be taken away or used as a basis for evidence, although the inspector may comment in your evaluation in their evidence.

- Where childminders work alone e.g. without an assistant, the inspector may observe a specific activity planned by the childminder and discuss the aims and learning objectives of the activity, this would then be followed up after the activity discussing what the child has gained from the experience and what their next steps would be.

The inspector tracking children as part of the inspection

During an inspection an inspector will track at least two children during their time in the setting. This will help them decide how well the setting meets individual needs, facilitates next steps and monitors progress. As part of this process the inspector will want to look at the tracked children's records e.g. learning journey and talk to the relevant key carers.

Preparation

This can be quite a daunting prospect for practitioners, so it is essential that the leader in the setting prepares staff for this, to boost confidence. This is achieved by:

- Including tracking of children and questioning as part of the staff observation and supervision cycle.

- Ensuring staff are confident in the planning cycle involved.

- Ensuring all staff are confident and up-to-date in their knowledge of the EYFS.

- That there are robust systems in place for monitoring the educational programme.

How the inspector will select the children

The inspector must track a minimum of two children, this will increase where there are a wide range of children, where children are in different rooms, where there are distinct groups of children and in larger settings.

They will identify children who have attended the setting for a reasonable amount of time, so that starting points have been established and progress has been evaluated. In the sample of tracked children, the inspector may include:

- A baby.

- A funded two-year-old.

- A boy and girl who are soon to transfer to school.

- Children the provision identifies as having differing abilities.

- A looked after child, if applicable.

- A child with disabilities and/special educational needs.

- A child who speaks English as an additional language.

- A boy/and or a girl from any groups who may be disadvantaged.

What evidence will the tracking include?

The inspector will need to collect evidence to go alongside their observations of the tracked child, this will include:

- Observations, assessments and planning for each child including starting points assessment and the progress check at two if applicable. They will evaluate the accuracy of the assessments and how well the children's next steps in learning are planned.

- Discussion with the child's key person about the child and their progress.

- They will look ay records the setting has that show how the child's progress has been tracked and include any concerns about development in the prime and/or specific areas of learning.

What will they observe the tracked child doing?

To help support the evaluations made, based on the evidence as detailed above, they will observe the following in relation to the child:

- The range of activities the child takes part in, considering if they are solitary, with others, self-initiated or adult-led.

- The quality and appropriateness of adults' interventions and interactions.

- The level of challenge available for the child in relation to their age/stage of development.

Assessment by the inspector of children's progress

The inspector needs to determine if the children are making progress and how well this is tracked and monitored. Children's progress relates mainly to the ability of the practitioners to identify individual needs and appropriate next steps and how this is demonstrated in knowledge and understanding of each child's learning and development.

The assessment of children's progress will begin from their starting points, taking into account how long they have been at the setting and how often they attend, their individual needs, looking at how the provision gathers information about what the children know and their progress towards the early learning goals.

The inspector will use the evidence they have gathered to evaluate how well the provider and practitioners know the children, understand them and the progress they are making. They will also want to see whether the adults have appropriately high expectations for the children and if children the gaps for children who are disadvantaged are narrowing and if children are at their expected levels of development.

The inspector will also consider the following as part of the assessment:

- Practitioner and provider/manager and practitioner understanding and knowledge of the EYFS.

- How and when parents/carers are asked for information about their child's development and how often summaries of their observations of children are shared with parents and the setting plans for reviewing progress at age two.

- Can practitioners reliably identify those children whose learning and development is not at the expected developmental band, either because they are working above or below the expected level and what is being done to support these children.

- How the SENCO is involved where there are concerns about a child.

- Any changes made to activities/resources/routines/the environment as a result of observations and evaluations of the impact of those changes.

After the inspection

help gain an insight into the experience and impact of change.

'Effects of change' questionnaire

Think of any changes you have experienced.

- How did you feel?

- How would you have preferred to experience the change (if negative) OR what made the change successful (if positive)?

- Why do you think someone introduced the change in the first place?

- Was it what you wanted or needed?

- Should your opinions count? Why?

When a change is planned or introduced the first thing that people ask themselves is how will this change affect me? This is particularly relevant if the change is presented to them with no discussion or explanation.

Change that is to be implemented after an inspection concerns everyone and therefore should involve everyone. This is essential if the change is going to be implemented successfully and have a positive impact on the setting. Even if the only involvement is being part of a discussion about how to move forward and work to implement action points.

For people to be accepting of change you need to be able to answer how the change will affect them as well as involve them to some degree in

---

> **Remember:** it may take up to three weeks to receive confirmation of your official Ofsted outcome.

Your inspection is over, so what should you do apart from breathe a huge sigh of relief? First and most importantly celebrate the successes of the inspection and identified areas of strength. This should involve every member of staff, as they will have all contributed to this. Make sure you tell the parents and carers of the children in your setting and why not generate some positive publicity by contacting your local paper?

Once the euphoria and sense of relief is over, you will need to sit down quietly without any distractions and read the report and identify what is being said. Regardless of the grading outcome of the inspection, there will be changes that you should implement as part of the setting's

continual development. This includes settings with an outstanding grading.

This might be particularly difficult if your inspection didn't go well or you were unhappy with the outcome. Your first impulse reaction might be to blame Ofsted, to blame yourself or another member of staff. It may take a while to be able to look at action points and outcomes with the perspective required. It is essential you reach the point of objectivity to be able to move forward. Don't blame anyone, including yourself, instead work on moving forward.

Part of moving forward is bound to involve change. By nature we are resistant to change so managers and leaders in settings need to look carefully at how they implement this change.

To begin with, it might be useful to answer questions in the box below to the planning of the change. This involvement helps to ensure that the change is implemented successfully and that the action points become part of practice.

Reasons for a resistance to change

- A desire not to loose something of value.

- A misunderstanding of the change and its implications.

- A belief that is doesn't make sense.

- A low tolerance for change – fear of not being able to develop new skills and behaviour required of them.

Managing successful change

- Keep the lines of communication open.

- If you can consult with the team, do.

- Be prepared to listen to concerns and respond appropriately.

- Give explanations and reasons.

- Ensure the team know the benefits and implications of the change and specifically how it affects their job role.

- Be honest about the expected effect of change.

- Review the effect of change after implementation.

To implement the change effectively and monitor the process of implementation and the outcome, you need to set Specific, Measurable, Achievable, Realistic and Time-bound (SMART) targets and devise an action plan, as discussed in the chapter on reflective practice.

Moving forward after an inspection is essential, the temptation will be to sit back and think 'oh we don't need to worry about that for another three years.' For any development of practice and skills to become embedded in the day-to-day you need to start as soon as possible. This will then help to ensure you reap the benefits at your next inspection. Most importantly, it means that you are providing the best possible early years experience for the children who attend your setting.

Remember to inform Ofsted if…

- There is a change of leader/person in charge in your setting, even if this is only temporary e.g. maternity leave.

- If there is a change of any address at which you provide childcare.

- If there is any significant event that is likely to affect the suitability of any person, who has reached the age of 16 and lives or works on the premises, to be in contact with children.

- The injury, serious accident or death of a child occurs whilst they are receiving registered childcare.

- The injury, serious accident or death to any other person on the premises on which the registered childcare is provided.

- If a child receiving childcare has a sudden serious illness.

- If there is any allegation of serious harm to or abuse of a child committed:

  ☐ By a person caring for children on the premises, whether the allegation relates to harm or abuse that occurred on those premises or elsewhere.

  ☐ By any person, where the allegation relates to harm or abuse that occurred on the premises.

- If there is any incident of food poisoning affecting two or more children cared for on the premises.

- If you wish to change the terms of your registration e.g. increase the number of children you care for.

Additionally, if you are a childminder, inform Ofsted if...

- A person in your household turns 16.

- You employ an assistant.

- An adult moves in or out of your house.

- You wish to build an extension to your house.

- It is essential to inform Ofsted of any of the above, as failure to do so is likely to impact on the outcome of an inspection.

- There is an explanation of what you may need to do to meet the requirements of the EYFS and how you can further improve the quality of your provision.

- Finally, a description of the inspector's judgements on the three outcomes.

With thoughtful preparation and using this book, your EYFS inspection can be a positive and stress-free experience. Remember also, with or without an inspection we can always develop and improve our practice and aim to provide the best service possible.

Inspection reports

The format for inspection reports has changed – they are now much clearer to read and give indicators of what you are doing well and where you can improve the develop your practice.

- The top of the report will clearly identify what grade you got for each of the three outcomes and your overall grade.

- There will then be a series of bullet points stating what is working well in your setting.

- Followed by the reason why you are not yet at a higher grade. If you are Outstanding, this section is omitted.

- There will be a list of what the inspector did during the visit e.g. what they observed, if they spoke to any parents, what paperwork they looked at and anything else they checked.

Further resources

Publications

Confident, Capable and Creative: Supporting Boys' Achievements (DCSF, 2007).

Inclusion Development Programme: Supporting Children with Speech, Language and Communication Needs – Guidance for Practitioners in the Early Years Foundation Stage (DCSF, 2008).

Key Elements of Effective Practice (KEEP) (DFES, 2005).

Safeguarding and Child Protection in the Early Years (Practical Pre-School Books, 2012).

Social and Emotional Aspects of Development: Guidance for Practitioners Working in the Early Years Foundation Stage (DCSF, 2008).

Supporting Children Learning English as an Additional Language (DCSF, 2007).

The Criminal Records Bureau Code of Practice and Explanatory Guide.

The Data Protection Act 2003.

The Disability Discrimination Act 2005.

The Early Years Foundation Stage in Practice (Practical Pre-School Books, revised 2012).

The Vetting and Barring Scheme (Independent Safeguarding Authority, 2009).

Childcare Groups: A Passion to be Outstanding (Ofsted, 2009).

Childminders: A Passion to be Outstanding (Ofsted, 2009).

Progress Matters: Reviewing and Enhancing Young Children's Development (DSCF, 2009).

Every Child A Talker: Guidance for Early Language Lead Practitioners (DSCF, 2009).

Building Futures: Believing in Children – A Focus on Provision for Black Children in the Early Years (DSCF, 2009).

Good Practice Guides – continually updated (www.ofsted.gov.uk).

Early Years Observation and Planning in Practice (Practical Pre-School Books, revised 2012).

Websites

www.foundationyears.org.uk

www.ofsted.gov.uk

www.education.gov.uk

Notes

Notes

Notes